May God bless
in all life's adventures!!

In This Together

A Collection of Sights and Insights
on Life and Love

by Louise R. Shaw

In This Together

Text and Photography ©1998 by Louise R. Shaw
Design by Toni Mertin, tmdesigns, Salt Lake City, Utah

———

Published by Capes to Canyons Press
P.O. Box 711533
Salt Lake City, Utah 84171-1533

———

———

Special thanks to:
Lora Cuykendall, Frances Richardson,
Annette and Sherwin Howard and Daren Shaw for sharing their expertise.
My family for providing unending inspiration.

———

ISBN # 0-9663592-0-8
Library of Congress Catalog Card Number: 98-92637

Living

No limits.

The sea extends forever

The sand goes on and on

The sky stretches to eternity

And so can I.

I can think about life

I can do cartwheels at the coast.

I've never been able to do cartwheels.

Not when I was 10 and all the other girls were pretending they were cheerleaders. Not when I was 15 and all the other girls were cheerleaders.

But at the coast, I can do cartwheels.

They're not pretty.

When you've lived to beyond 30 without doing a cartwheel, they're not going to be pretty.

They're not something to show off to the world – even your own children look around anxiously when you're that old, hoping no one has noticed their crazy mother.

But I can do them. At the coast.

I can think about life at the coast.

At home I'm too busy thinking about PTA and the next den meeting or dinner or what I need to remember not to forget the next time I buy groceries.

But at the coast, those thoughts are washed away by the pounding of the surf and my mind is clear to think about life and love and heaven and forever.

I have to go to the coast as often as possible. It is there, as I sit and watch the waves crash in the surf and the clouds dance across the sky, while my children build sand castles and fly kites and collect shells, that I am renewed and refilled.

For my sister, it's the stars. Late at night, after her kids are in bed, she stares up into the night sky and her soul is filled.

For my husband, it's the mountains. Skiing or hiking brings him relaxation and rejuvenation and a chance for reflection.

The beauties of the earth and skies weren't put here just for us to build on or drive past or glance at or ignore.

They can give us strength we never knew we had and peace we didn't know existed.

We just have to go there.

Leave behind the pace, the pull, the drain of everyday… and go there.

Abandon the tasks, the trivia, and even the reserve… just go there.

It's a strange sort of freedom.

We're free to speak, to worship, to write, to assemble, to bear arms and to petition the government when necessary.

But we're not free to walk alone after dark, to leave our house unlocked or to let our children play alone in the front yard.

We're free to do what we choose, but we're not free from those who choose to do that which is wrong.

Reading the paper isn't much fun anymore.

Stories of rape, abuse and murder climb off the pages and unwittingly into our minds, demanding to be read.

We are all drawn to the horror stories, hoping to find something that will distance us from the tragic things that happen to others, and knowing they will make us more aware of how to avoid similar dangers.

But those stories also make us less free as we become more afraid.

Afraid to sleep with a breeze from an open window. Afraid to let someone see the address on our checks. Afraid to open our door to strangers.

For mothers, that fear is multiplied.

We are afraid to let our kids walk to a nearby friend's house. Afraid to take

There is no more critical job

them to parks or leave them at pre-schools. Unwilling to trust even a friendly face since professionals warn us to be wary of baby-sitters, teachers, clergymen and doctors, and even relatives.

So who's left to trust?

School curriculum once included extras like how to escape a fire. Now our children are taught how to avoid kidnappers and the AIDS virus and how to say "no" when someone touches them in the wrong place.

But even if we can protect our children from danger, we can't protect them from the fear of it.

I hated being told of a rape in our neighborhood. I didn't want to know – it made me nervous to walk the two blocks from a friend's house to my own at dusk, causing my heart to pound every time a car would pass or some movement was perceived in a dark shadow.

I hated being afraid. But my mother knew I needed to be aware.

And now, as a mother, I face the same task. Do I warn my children and pass along that fear, or do I risk having them find out the hard way?

I fought the inevitable answer for a long time, wanting to keep my children innocent, trusting and carefree. But I also had to keep them safe.

They have to know, and they have to limit their own freedoms in order to avoid the dangers in our world.

It's freedom we have. But freedom with fear.

The answer isn't in bigger jails or tougher judges or stiffer penalties.

It's not in money thrown at education programs or child fingerprinting or "Say 'no' to drugs" campaigns.

It's not in more policemen or more alternative schools or more restrictive laws or bigger homeless shelters.

We will only be truly free when every individual in our society recognizes and honors the personal freedom of every other individual. When respect replaces resentment, love replaces lust, values replace vices.

When every single citizen knows that their rights end where another's freedom begins.

They will not learn that from the schools, the government, the press or their peers.

They will only learn it from the mothers and the fathers in the quiet of a home.

There is no more critical job in the whole, wide world.

She wasn't quite big enough for the merry-go-round, and the teeter-totter doesn't work for just one.

Her two-year-old legs weren't long enough to get her on the jungle gym and the slide appeared way too high for so wary an adventurer.

Without help, she couldn't sit in the customary manner on the swing, so she tried balancing her pudgy tummy on the swing's plastic seat, dangling her arms on one side and her legs on the other.

She soon found she could lift up her feet a little and swing freely. Gradually she built more confidence and in short order was swinging high, kicking her legs, flailing her arms, twisting around in the air and squealing in delight.

She swung for a very long time, oblivious to others' activities around her, and only leaving one swing to perfect the same moves on another.

Her delight in her new discovery was exciting to see.

There was no envy of those who were taller or braver or more skilled. There was no embarrassment that she couldn't climb as high or resentment that her legs couldn't reach as far.

There was only delight

There was only sincere pleasure in her newfound skill and true enjoyment of the moment.

Watching her made it easy to know:

Having fun on your tummy on a swing is every bit as fulfilling as having fun any other old way.

Being your best at something you love is every bit as grand as any other accomplishment.

I think it's a nut, I think that it fell.

This is your home, you know it well.

I'll touch it, turn it, check for a smell.

Then it's yours 'cause you want it. I can tell.

"We're all going to die out here!"

"We're lost!"

"No, this is the way, over here."

"Yikes – poison oak!"

"We're all going to die out here."

"What time does the next class start? We're going to miss the next class."

"I'm hungry."

"Are you OK?"

"Ouch – watch out for that branch."

"This is the way back."

"No, this is the way back."

"Let's go this way."

"We're all going to die."

It was a sampling of humanity, the little Cub Scout Troop trampling through the wooded area behind the day camp.

There were the adventurers, the worriers, the leaders, the conscientious clock-watchers, the cautious, the pessimists.

All eleven of them together, bushwhacking their way through the unknown, exposing their personalities in the process.

And I traipsed along after them, making sure that if we did get lost, we all got lost together and that nobody really did die and that there really wasn't poison oak and that we really would make it back to class when necessary, and at the same time listening to the variety of sentiments and concerns expressed as we trekked.

We weren't really in any danger. In leaving the heavily wooded area, we would have come out at either the city park or a cow pasture.

Still, it was high adventure for the little eight- to ten-year-old troopers.

We'd been trying to get along all day as those who wanted to be funny disrupted demonstrations and those who wanted to make sure the rules were followed told everybody else what they were doing wrong and those who wanted to be bold fought with those who considered themselves bolder.

It was the ultimate challenge for someone like me, who by nature requires everybody to be happy and nice and get along.

But it wasn't the first time I've had to deal with myriad personalities.

In my own home, the scope of individuality and the situations that result make an interesting study.

One would expect children born of the same parents to exhibit similar personality traits. Or boys to be one way and girls to be another way. Or opposites to be divided into two categories.

But I've come to learn that having four children means having four distinctly opposite personalities to learn to live with and love.

In my family alone you will find the sensitive, quiet child; the sharp, meticulous child; the mild-mannered, loving child, and the loud, controlling child (not necessarily in that order). This variety makes it impossible to ever perfect whatever parenting skills we ever may have thought we had.

Potty training for one child was done with M&Ms as a reward. Another only pulled through when Ernie and Bert heaped praise and support. Another only graduated from diapers when he felt like it, regardless of the reward or the satisfaction.

With each child, with each lesson, a new strategy had to be developed.

One child learned from a slight reprimand, another fell apart when given a slight reprimand. For yet another, a slight reprimand meant absolutely nothing.

There was the child who lived for books and a child who would rather go to bed early than read. There was a child who wanted to ride a two-wheeler at two and another who had no interest at six.

Each had different tastes, different abilities and different distractions.

Like those Cub Scouts.

Like people.

The bold entrepreneurs, the insightful teachers, the successful inventors, the creative artisans – or for that matter the bold artisans, the successful entrepreneurs, the creative teachers and the insightful inventors – create a worldwide kind of synergism.

Differences make for continual advancements, unusual insights and occasional surprises.

You're different from me, but my life is more interesting because I know you.

Too old for a nap.

And not tired anyway.

Just want to watch Sesame Stre…

Training wheels would solve the problem.

Or so we thought.

It was our end-of-school-start-of-summer family vacation and we were all excited about exploring together the bike trails in and around Central Oregon.

In past years, it had taken two big bikes pulling trailers to get us around, but this time everybody was old enough to manage his or her own wheels. For those who hadn't mastered the required balance, my husband and I decided the solution was as simple as training wheels.

On they went and off we headed, with a short explanation on pressing one pedal down and then the other, just like with Big Wheels only higher.

Around the corner and down the block they pedaled, my husband and I right behind, smiling at how easy it was and how fun it would be.

But soon our self-congratulation ended as our children whirred ahead to an unanticipated slope and we realized we'd forgotten to mention something fairly significant.

Moments later, as we plucked them from the sagebrush, we shook our heads at such oversight.

Imagine teaching how to go without teaching how to stop. Besides being short-sighted, it was downright dangerous.

And even training wheels couldn't compensate.

We'd forgotten something fairly significant

I've never been very good at stopping.

It was always full speed ahead, one foot down and then the other as fast as you can pedal. I could help out here, I can master that, I can take on the next thing and I'll do every one 100 percent. If something was right and good, I would find the time and work everything and everyone else around my schedule.

But then I crashed.

That little mechanism inside my body that grew ever more insistent with every passing year, said, "If you won't apply the brakes, I will."

One time it sent a message via my back. Though I'd just had my fourth child, I was sure I could exercise hard and get back in shape right away, just as I had after previous deliveries.

But this time my body thought differently.

And as I lay flat on my back for three straight days, I had to admit there are times to slow things down.

Times to lie down in the sagebrush and have a good cry and then look up and see the trees overhead that you hadn't noticed before or the squirrel gnawing on the nut nearby that you'd have driven right by had you been on top of things.

Times to breathe deeply and think clearly and pray sincerely before climbing back up on that bike and getting back at it all.

Times when the hurt becomes the healer.

Summer is my chance

If ever I have a nervous breakdown it will be during soccer season.

Soccer season is when I'm most likely to be staring at blank walls long into the night, wondering who I am and how I got where I am now and wishing I were somewhere else.

Soccer season is the season I get tired without doing anything, angry without anyone crossing me and depressed when everything's going on schedule.

It's not just because I have two or more children playing soccer in any given season.

It's not just because their coaches choose different days and different times and different schools to have their practices.

It's not just because every Saturday for eight weeks is spent running from one game to the other – or worse yet, trying to watch two games in two different places at the same time.

It's because soccer season marks the beginning of the end of my freedom.

After nearly three months of carefree fun, of hiking and swimming and camping and traveling and exploring and discovering, the freedom ends and the demands begin.

It's usually a phone call a week into August.

"Come to a meeting…, practices begin…, be sure and buy…," say the voices on the other end.

And three weeks ahead of the school district's already crowded schedule, I'm going to stores for shin guards, finding out about how parents should and should not act at games, and beginning the grand tour de schools that each season entails. Unless I can come up with an excuse – and I usually do – like a necessary final trip to the mountains or the coast.

But sooner or later it catches up with me and I'm back at the wheel with soccer balls and water bottles rolling around in the car.

And a pit in my stomach.

Summer is my chance to introduce my children to the world.

They can read about it during the school year.

They can write essays about it using the essays they read in the school library's encyclopedia as a resource. They can draw pictures of the pictures they've seen in magazines or on the overhead projector during school.

But in the summertime, I get to let them see it, feel it, taste it and touch it.

Like octopuses, newts, glacial lakes, waterfalls, Ferris wheels, volcanoes and the bunnies at state fairs.

Like parks and playgrounds, campfires and craters, waves and wildflowers, rowboats and rainstorms.

In the summertime, we can run through the sprinkler all afternoon and listen to crickets all night, or we can head out to adventures in the vast unknown.

14

But as August closes, the luxury of leisure time ends, and my own personal depression sets in.

I don't have anything against school. I think it's grand that children can go somewhere and learn how to get along with their

peers and their teachers, how to make friends and how to obey somebody else's rules.

And the fact that they learn mathematics and reading makes it all the better.

Still, I fight the loss of the time I have with my children. The time I can use to love them, to answer their questions about dams and deer, dandelions and drudgery. The time we have to discover our world together.

It is likely an extension of the loss I have felt as my children have grown old enough not only for school and sports, but for parties and friends and lessons that take them away from home so much of the time.

In the early years, our schedule was our own. We could eat what we wanted to and when we felt like it, we could go to museums or fly kites, we could clean house together or watch a movie instead.

Now, I'm scheduled. I'm assigned, I'm regulated.

And while I'm sure I'll adjust, rise to the challenge and fall in line as I should, it may take me a bit longer than most.

Because there are things more important than soccer practices and team meetings.

There are bedtime stories and family dinners and quiet evenings at home.

And until I can balance the demands of the world and the needs of a family, I may be found sitting somewhere, staring.

When chocolate pudding is served at our house, a peculiar thing happens.

First someone points out the window and says something like, "Look – a five-legged dog!"

Of those gullible enough to look, one will turn back unrewarded, only to find a spoonful of pudding missing from his or her bowl. Meanwhile, the one who pointed out the oddity will be swallowing. And smiling.

Then someone else usually spots a monster in the kitchen, and as curious heads turn, another spoonful of pudding disappears from one bowl and ends up in another's mouth.

I know it's uncivilized, and unsanitary, and impolite, and though I frown disapproval at the perpetrators (especially my husband who started it) there's no stopping it.

It's a tradition.

Those familiar with the game "Duck, duck , goose," would have noticed a slight variation at our house during our "Duck, duck, goose" years.

Rather than the better-known wording, those who circled the circle tapping people on the head, were more likely to say something like "Orange, orange – apple," or "Tyrannosaur, tyrannosaur, – Tyrannosaurus Rex," or "Clean diaper, clean diaper – dirty diaper."

I know it's silly, but it's much more entertaining than the old method.

It's also tradition.

Traditions can start up spontaneously, be transplanted from other families, or inherited from your own.

I brought some traditions from my childhood family to my parenthood after marriage. Some worked – like ice cream after every meal (my dad is a dairy scientist), singing "Old Dan Tucker" in the car, the tri-fold creature game (too hard to explain), and a sibling slumber party on Christmas Eve.

Others didn't.

It's a tradition

Like potato chips at Thanksgiving.

My grandmother always had potato chips out on a little TV tray before the Thanksgiving feast. That way we'd snack a bit here and a bit there while the final turkey preparations were underway, and never be hungry enough to pester about when dinner was going to be ready.

Some years ago I set out before our holiday guests a bowl of chips and a dip.

"What's that?" my husband exclaimed in disbelief. "Potato chips before turkey dinner? And you'll probably be serving Twinkies after the pumpkin pie!"

He was quite adamant about the impropriety, so I abandoned that tradition without any real loss.

On other traditions, I stand firm.

It was traditional in my family to take "sight-seeing vacations." That is, you started at one point, stopped at every museum, historical marker, visitors' center and cheese factory (remember my dad) until you got to the final point, and then you came home a different route, stopping again for points of geological or historical significance.

My husband came into our marriage with a vastly different view of vacationing. Vacations, to my husband, are going to some quiet spot – preferably a warm beach – for rest and relaxation. Physical activity such as swimming, snorkeling, hiking or biking is permitted. Museums most generally are not.

It has taken a good many years of vacationing together to work out a manageable compromise – especially when it became evident that my children inherited the vacationing gene from my husband and vastly prefer relaxing outdoor activities to visitors' centers.

Nevertheless, we have successfully added play days to sight-seeing trips and topped off relaxing trips with a gallery, natural wonder or cheese factory (as long as it serves ice cream on the side).

Traditions can be silly, significant or spontaneous, inherited, invented or adapted.

They provide a link from the past to the future, and give roots to children who are often more preoccupied with their wings.

We're in this together

We can jump, we can run

Higher and faster

In sand and in sun.

We're free and life's beckoning

Hold on to my hand,

We're in this together

Let's make it fun!

Loving

On opening a certain drawer in a certain little boy's room, you'll notice the absence of the usual socks, shirts and shorts.

Instead there are game pieces, stickers, a ruler, a puppet, an alligator eraser, Legos, masking tape, scotch tape, a Ninja Turtles night light, book marks, a toy clock and a postcard his aunt sent from Austria.

It's his "treasure drawer."

The place where everything special is carefully accumulated.

And when the drawer proves too small, overflow wooden puzzles, the stamp set from the cereal box, the toy his little sister

Mothers are funny sometimes

won at a party and the Trix he was too full to finish can be found in the drawers with his pajamas and underwear.

Shells, pieces of colored yarn, rocks, drawings and cards are treasures that can be found in little secret stashes in each one of my children's rooms.

Over time, each has developed a considerable collection of items they cherish above all.

Every year before school starts, I enter my oldest daughter's bedroom with grocery bags in hand, generally filling the first three with art and craft creations made from shoe boxes, yarn, popsicle sticks or old fabric, and no longer considered valuable. Two more grocery bags hold items that may have been precious to her but that really belong in other rooms like masking tape

(again?), old tennis balls, and the Draw Four's from the UNO game. The real valued items – the China doll, the agates, the globe piggy bank and the fluorescent friendship bracelets, remain behind to adorn shelves or to be neatly arranged in special drawers.

Like my children, I too have lots of treasures. Mine, in fact, fill the house.

I have a bowling trophy I bought to taunt my husband when I beat him for the first time at anything. I have two clay creations and two heart–shaped candle holders made by little kindergarten hands over the years as gifts on Mother's Day.

A half-made violin carved by my grandfather has a prominent place in my den, reminding me of his rough-around-the-edges personality. A delicate gold mirror and brush lie on my bathroom counter, bringing thoughts of my refined and delicate grandmother, to whom they once belonged.

To some they may be curious decor or even clutter.

To me they are treasures.

I spoke once with my mother about these irreplaceable items and their value to me.

"Oh," she said, apparently thinking of me as I thought of my son and his collections, "they're just things."

Mothers are funny sometimes.

Just yesterday we received a postcard from her in the mail.

It began, "Dear Treasures…"

You're new to me and I'm new to you.

You look different from me and I do things different from you.

You've seen things I never will and I'll see things you wouldn't believe.

You're at one end of the journey and I'm at the other.

You're new to me and I'm new to you.

But I like you.

One day when everything was quiet, I got down on the floor and looked up at things from the angle of my baby's gaze.

Everyone was so big and everything seemed so far away and it was so disappointing when the one who was speaking to you walked away to something else.

One day, just out of curiosity, I crawled under the bed where my four-year-old son would hide after being reprimanded. It was lonely and quiet there, and I wondered as I stared up at the boards that hold the mattress up, if anyone really loved me.

One day, I wondered how it felt when someone else always got to choose where to sit in the movie theater and decide when to buy the popcorn. And then I knew why my six-year-old could get so frustrated.

One day I wondered how it felt to have everyone walking farther and faster than

It was lonely and quiet there

me and to fear being left behind in a place I'd never been before. And then I understood why my little two-year-old would run with all her might while screaming, "Wait 'or me," at the top of her lungs.

There is power in being a parent.

I can walk away from a playful baby to get the clothes out of the dryer or answer the telephone.

I can send a child who loves people and needs to be loved to his room, where he is even more alone because those last words spoken to him were so harsh.

I can decide where to sit, what to buy and how fast to walk.

I can choose when to have dinner, when friends can play, what TV shows can be watched and when bedtime should come.

Sometimes though, it's good to put on different shoes, be they booties, jellies or Sesame Street Keds.

When I do that, different things become frustrating and scary. Different things become important. Different things become sad.

When I do that, I become different, too.

You look away...

To the kite, to the friend,

to the adventure, to the future.

I look at you...

To the child, to the woman

to the friend, to the future.

For my
infant son

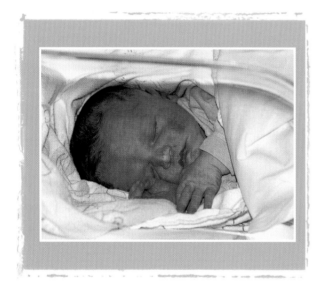

I suppose there will come a time
    when you'll push my kisses away like your big brother does now.
    when you'll stick your tongue out at me
    and say you hate me.
    when you'll say "no" to the requests I make of you
    and yell demands for a drink or a cookie of me.

But for now you are my sweet, cuddly baby boy,
    who lights up when our eyes meet
    and nestles in against my shoulder when weary.
    who gets his sole nourishment from my body
    and whose needs are understood by no one better than I.

We love each other, you and I.
    We accept each other no matter the hour of the day
    the style of clothing
    or the mood.

It won't always be that way.

Just now
    when you are newly mine and I am newly yours.
Just now
    as I caress your soft skin and vow to protect you from anyone
    or anything that could harm you.
Just now
    as you look into my eyes with those bright, searching, accepting eyes.
Just now
    as we build a bond of love that will take us through the years of "hate yous"
    and "leave me alones."
Just now
    as those who don't understand may say I'm spoiling you,
    I'm giving you love that you might not accept later
    but that will be yours forever.

Because you are my son.

For my son, age four

"My favorite color is green," he said out of the blue
    staring up at the older woman expectantly
    anxious for her response.
    "Green?" she said in obvious disdain, "that's about my least favorite color."
The smile on his face wilted only slightly
    but my heart sank.
A hidden request for acceptance
    was rejected.

"You're making it very difficult for me,"
    the very grown-up neighbor boy said as he walked off with another.
    "I played with you yesterday and today I don't want to play with you.
    "Now please leave me alone."
I sat helplessly as my four-year-old son sank to the floor.
Rejected openly.
I couldn't make the others play with him –
    that wouldn't count.
I couldn't make him happy to be left out –
    that wouldn't be natural.

When he was a baby it seemed my love and my arms could protect him from anything.
Even thoughtlessness.
As he grows I become ever more helpless
    as his world reaches beyond me
    to siblings, friends, relatives, classmates.

"I love you," I said
    when the others had gone and the tears had quieted.
"I know," he retorted angrily.
"How come you always say that?"

So you'll always know,
    I thought as I held him,
    that no matter who says what about you
    or to you
    and no matter in what ways you fail or succeed
    that I'll always love you.

Because I always will.

Little girls watch

Little girls watch as
    in a gown of white,
    she turns this way for the camera
    and tilts her chin that way
    and glows.

Little girls whisper as
    thinking no one will notice,
    she smiles and winks
    at the man who just today became
    her husband.

Little girls wait as
    each individually but all in one,
    they dream of the day
    when they will be white
    and winking
    and wonderful.

He reads and I write.

The flurry of bedtime stories
  and goodnight kisses ended,
  only silence remains
  waiting to be interrupted by one last cry of the baby,
  a toddler's request for a drink
  or the final swish of the dishwasher.

Finally no one requires
  results from him
  or response
  from me.

His talk of deadlines and details,
  mine of diapers and demands
  subsides.

He reads and I write.

Together
  in a world we share
  separately.

Together, separately

He wears the shorts. I have the parka.

At first glance they didn't go together.

They were a walking mismatch. A visual anomaly.

All the other twosomes wandering past our spot in the sand had somehow fit.

Some passed in blue jeans and jackets. Others both had shorts and shirts from Eddie Bauer. Some whizzed by, riding bikes and wearing pants with cuffs rolled up. Other couples sported similar leather jackets, dyed hair and dangly earrings.

But this couple didn't match.

He was wearing shorts and a tank top. She was in long pants and a warm parka. He walked along in sandals. Her feet were protected by warm socks and solid shoes. He looked confident and comfortable. She looked cold and conservative.

It was an eye-catching irregularity and our curiosity kept them in our sights for a bit longer than the others.

It was a sunny day, and anyone looking out a window from a cozy room would surely opt to wear shorts for a stroll on the beach.

That explained his attire.

Yet it was also a windy day – so windy that even bright sunshine couldn't get the thermometer to rise above 60 degrees.

Thus, her parka.

And that's how we came to the conclusion that this unusual couple had a remarkable relationship.

It wasn't the arm he put around her after they had passed. It was the clothes that didn't match.

Relationships often start out with each party trying to "match" the other. My husband likes tennis and skiing, so when we first began dating, I got myself a tennis racket and snow skis and learned to do both.

It was great fun at first. I enjoyed tennis, whether I won or lost, and it was absolute heaven for me to be floating through the peaceful majesty of a snow-covered mountain on skis.

It took less than a year for my husband to tell me that I ruined his tennis game. Having someone wimpily hit a ball back gave him no chance to improve his already-advanced skills. Someone who has fun "win or lose" is not the kind of killer partner you'd want in a doubles tournament either.

We skied together off and on for years before we had to go our separate ways on the slopes as well.

He was too good and too fast. I was too cautious and timid.

He wears the shorts. I have the parka.

There are still lots of things we enjoy doing together despite our differing tastes.

I go to his kind of concerts and he goes to mine, we take turns choosing which restaurants to try, and go to each other's kind of movies.

But then there are times when I let him be him and he lets me be me without compromise or condescension.

When you think about it, it's amazing marriage has remained in vogue for so long.

You take two people who disagree on everything from how to squeeze a toothpaste tube to how much to spend on a car, run them through a quick ceremony and send them out to sleep together, pay bills together and raise children together, and you're asking for trouble.

Especially now that chores are no longer preassigned.

But as dating partners and then marriage partners grow together and then grow in different directions, it becomes apparent that in a really solid relationship, the individuals who make up the pair can go back to being individuals without threatening the pair.

It doesn't happen over night.

It hadn't happened yet for the young couple I met at a party recently.

They were delighted to have found a solution to their disagreement over television sports. He can watch all he wants as long as he pays her a dollar an hour for the privilege. She's looking forward to a new wardrobe, he's glad to have peace and quiet, and I'm thinking such a "compromise" had best be short-lived.

Sometimes it takes longer than others to work the differences out, as with a friend of mine who was planning a surprise party for her husband of 10 years.

"He'll kill me," she said. "He hates parties and being the center of attention."

"Then why are you throwing a surprise party for him," was the obvious question.

"Because I like them," she said, "and I'm in charge of his birthday. And when it's my birthday, he can take me out to dinner for two at a quiet restaurant the way he likes to celebrate."

Such different people in a marriage. Such difficult issues to resolve. Such delightful conflicts until their resolutions bring about mutual understanding and respect.

And then two people can love being unique and individual, together.

I don't often meet a problem I don't want to solve, an owee I don't want to kiss better or a sad book I don't want to make happy.

Yet sobbing through the final pages of *Uncle Tom's Cabin*, I knew nothing could be done to remedy the heart-rending

She crumbled to a heap

conclusion. It was tragedy based on reality and couldn't be happily-ever-aftered away. Louisa May Alcott ruined my day when she didn't have Jo marry Laurie after spending most of *Little Women* developing their relationship. But by the end of the book, everybody seemed happy enough so I let it go.

However, one ending had to be redone for my own peace of mind:

"Frankly my dear, I don't give a damn."
She crumbled to a heap on the floor as he
slammed the door and marched down the steps.

A world of troubles came crashing down on her tiny figure at the base of the tall staircase. The war, the wounded, the deaths, the poverty, Bonnie, the unborn baby, Melanie, and now... now Rhett.

How could she live without Rhett — the one who'd teased her, helped her, loved her, saved her. She'd been a fool not to admit it. All those years she'd used him, taunted him, wanting what she couldn't have until she got it, rejecting what she had until it was no longer hers. But now she had to admit: It was Rhett she loved.

"I've lost too much," she told herself. But he'd lost too. The confidence he had always had in every situation had now turned to bitterness. Bitterness because of how she had hurt him.

She ran to the door, flew down the stairs and into the dark mist. Running blindly toward the river, she called his name madly, desperate not to lose him now that she'd only just found him.

"Rhett," she screamed, as she ran. Only footsteps rang out in the darkness.

"Rhett," she shouted almost hysterically, running faster as she saw his shape on the bridge. "Rhett."

He stopped dead, not turning or responding.

"Rhett," she said, catching up but standing just behind as she regained her breath and waited for his reaction.

"I know now that I love you. I will always love you. I have always loved you. Please forgive me."

He didn't move but straightened his tall frame as he looked ahead into nothingness.

"I've been such a fool. I'm sorry.

"I love you."

Then slowly he turned, looking angrily into her eyes, then deeply into her soul.

She returned his challenge, beseeching him with her determined eyes to believe in her again — or for the first time. Telling him silently that they could heal their wounds together.

Tears started down her cheeks.

Rhett watched them fall.

Her heavy breathing turned to deep sobs.

Rhett watched her cry.

The water swirled under the bridge. The mist curled around the solitary figures.

Then Rhett reached out slowly and took Scarlett's hand.

There. I feel better now.

Sights

Neat, huh Dad.

I knew what he was feeling.

As he stood there with his chin quivering, his lips pursed tightly and his eyes getting a little bit shimmery, I knew exactly what he wanted to do.

The little eight-year-old goalie had been ineffective in stopping no less than four goals from being kicked past him in the last five minutes.

He knew he had failed. He knew his teammates knew he had failed. And while his mom tried to smile bravery to him, and his coach told him it was OK and that he was doing a good job and that he should just keep it up, he knew his mom and his coach knew he had failed. And he just wanted to cry about it.

But he couldn't.

Eight-year-old boys can't cry in front of teammates and coaches and mothers. But their chins sometimes quiver and their lips sometimes are pursed a bit too tightly together and their eyes sometimes get just a tiny bit shimmery.

And some of us who have been there know just how they feel.

It's happened more than once to me. Tragic stories. Moving books, sad movies, happy movies, bad arguments or good commercials have all had their effect.

It was even during a basketball game that a commercial for I-don't-remember what came on and took the rug out from under me.

Here came a firefighter racing from a building, as the camera jumped from him to an anxious couple waiting outside. Back went the camera to his dangerous race down crashing steps and through flaming doors, then back to the couple.

Finally, he made it out, opened his coat to reveal a warm, safe and snug baby.

And as the action moved on to fancy cars and flashy beers and tight basketball games, I sat with tears running down my cheeks.

In the privacy of your own home, with good friends and a tolerant husband around, these things can be overlooked.

But sometimes it happens in public.

While society accepts tears in the dark of a movie theater at the end of a good movie, and claims that men can now prove their sensitivities by being emotional (which of course they wouldn't dare because they know society is just saying that), society doesn't know how to handle the sobbing that results at the print shop when a computer crash erases two hours of work, or the cries of anger at the department of motor vehicles when the woman who watched while the 200 people in front of her got licensed, is told she doesn't have the right paperwork.

And society certainly can't handle pregnant women. A pregnant woman not only cries when her husband looks at her sideways, but when the grocery store clerk tells her she is purchasing too many items to be in the express lane.

There are just some feelings that can't be shoved aside and pretended away but must be felt all the way.

Some may say that mind can control matter, but heart is an entirely different thing.

Moving books, sad movies and good commercials

It was done in shades of blue with a touch of peach here and there and when I first saw it, tears sprang to my eyes.

Something about the painting made me see beauty in something that had previously been just another duty.

patchwork pieces so patiently arranged in design and so warmly healing.

I knew just what had happened as I drank in the picture. She had heard his cries, wrapped him tightly in the warm quilt, told him everything would be OK

tears, I pass it in the dark and know that what I'm doing isn't a terrible inconvenience at all.

It took two years before my youngest slept through the night. I listened to all the advice from outsiders – let him cry, feed him yogurt or oatmeal, skip a nap, and on and on.

Then I realized that every moment during the day, we were surrounded by one or two or three others and their wants and needs and troubles. At night, just the two of us were together. My son and I.

Maybe life really is

The child was sound asleep in his mother's arms, his head on her shoulder, her cheek resting against his curly hair. Light from a nearby window was just beginning to chase the dark shadows away.

The rocking chair in the background was empty. Whatever his need, she had taken him in her arms without waiting to get to a more comfortable spot.

The quilt she held him in was further evidence of someone's love. The little

now, and rocked him gently until his fears and tears were quieted and he was once again safe and warm and asleep.

But though he sleeps, she does not. And as she holds him snugly, the faraway look in her eyes is evidence that she too is at peace.

I cut out the picture from the magazine, had it mounted, double-matted and framed and hung it right next to the door that leads from my room.

When I get up in the night to calm

It was then I decided that those few minutes together were not a chore or a pain or a sacrifice.

They were an act of love, a sweet service.

And then, as the woman in the painting in shades of blue, I felt peace.

$Snow$ on a mountain peak.

Ice on the lake.

Blue sky over a wintry scene.

Icing on the cake.

"Do you see that tree?"

There was no pulpit. No organ music, no choir. But it was a sermon just the same.

Conditions can't always be perfect, but timing is everything and this time I was standing over my kitchen stove working on dinner.

"John says he doesn't believe in God," said my seven-year-old son of his friend from next door whose name has been changed even though he's not innocent.

"Oh," I said, being careful not to drop the frying pan or let my face turn too bright a red. "What do you think?"

"I think I can believe what I see," he said, leaving me to grip even harder onto the pan and my emotions.

"Oh?" I said again, with deceptive reserve. "Do you see that tree out there?"

"Yes."

"Do you know who made it?"

"God?"

"That's right, and don't you ever forget it."

"Is Canada over the ocean?"

We talked about anger at lunch one day when my children were still young.

The subject came up because I had been angry and felt badly about it.

We had just run a "quick" errand, the baby was overly tired and fussy, and, while I wrestled with him to prepare him for a nap, the older kids opened a two-pound block of cheese and carved it to smithereens, dropping odd pieces on the floor I had spent an hour mopping that morning – where it was ground in by lingering feet.

It wasn't a furious anger. It was a resigned anger, which left the kids tiptoeing around, trying to find something to do that wouldn't set me off.

"I'm not going to eat any food before this lunch so you won't get angry," said the one who had close to a quarter pound of cheese in his stomach already.

But his sensitivity made me regret my insensitivity, so we discussed it over chicken noodle soup and crackers.

"I get angry sometimes when people make messes, or don't obey, or fight," I began. And everybody nodded.

"And when I'm angry, sometimes I yell or send you to your rooms or get frustrated and mumble to myself," I continued.

Again, nods all around.

"What makes you angry?" I asked my oldest son.

He told about people who lock him out of their rooms or take his toys, speaking, we all realized, of his older and younger sisters, respectively.

"What do you do when you get angry?" I asked. He kicks closed doors, he cries and he tries to hit people, we decided.

Then we talked about his older sister. She gets angry when younger siblings destroy her creations and when other people get angry with her. When she's angry, she hits and calls people stupid.

We all knew that their little sister gets angry when someone takes a toy of hers or won't include her in their play. She simply screams.

"It's OK to get angry," I said, after we recognized that we all did it. "But it's not OK if we're so angry we hurt people."

"What's this letter?" said my youngest daughter, more concerned about the shape of her noodle than the subject at hand.

"Capital I," I said, not bothering to explain that this was chicken noodle, not alphabet soup.

"But I want you to know," I said, returning to the discussion, "that even when I'm angry, I still love you."

I looked around to see how the point had been taken. My son made it quite clear:

"Is Canada over the ocean?"

I smiled all the way out to the car and then all the way home.

The young salesclerk in the discount shoe store had asked me if I was buying my new sandals to wear to the prom. It was a comment he'd made in jest during the course of the sale, but it made me smile.

Imagine, after all these kids and years – the prom!

I told my husband of the compliment that night, half wondering if he would become jealous, half hoping he'd tell me that I really do look young and that the gray strand of hair just to the left of my part really isn't that noticeable.

"Right," he said, unmoved. "Going to the prom as a chaperone, maybe."

I stopped smiling then.

As a chaperone. Complete with bad knee, over-wide hips and gray hair to the left of my part.

There was no fooling my husband.

My short-lived vanity vanished as I went back to fixing dinner, answering kids' questions, giving commands and feeling old.

It wasn't that I wanted to go to the prom. Those days of buying fancy dresses, hoping for the right date, getting the wrong date, the anticipation, the disappointments, the anxiety, the he-likes-me-but-I-like-another-guy-who-likes-another-girl, are ever-so-gratefully over.

It was just that I wanted to pretend I looked young enough to be a prom candidate.

The point here isn't how inconsiderate, rude and unthinking husbands can be. The point is how much a little compliment can

"Going to the Prom?"

lift spirits and instill a bright bit of confidence.

It was just a few days later that I took my children out to dinner at a casual restaurant. Their dad was out of town for a few days and I never cook dinner when I don't have to.

Throughout the meal I was conscious of a man across the aisle from my four busy children. He was an older, single gentleman, and I was sure the spilled JELL-O, occasional overly-loud comments and overall manners of my children must have annoyed him.

As we got up to leave, collecting our napkins and packages, I stooped to pick up the tromped-in fish fillet that my youngest had been unable to keep on his plate.

"What a good-looking family you have, young lady," he said.

My embarrassment turned into a quick smile as I thanked him, no longer impatient but proud.

Grandmothers, like that gentleman, are unsurpassed at finding the good. You don't have to be cute or smart for a grandmother to think you're both and tell you so. Coaches, in contrast, quite often do the opposite. No matter how hard you've practiced or how hard you're trying, there always seems to be something you're not doing yet and need to do soon.

Sometimes unknowingly, we become the supportive grandmother – or the dissatisfied coach.

I've seen the glow from a kind word honestly spoken. I've seen the hurt from a critical comment even well-intentioned.

I'll take the glow.

You can't see it from the road.

This view is hidden by the hills

and the trees

and the angles.

When you speed so swiftly past

you don't even know

you missed it.

You have to get out of your car

and walk until your heart is racing

and your face is beet red

and your legs are tired

and your shirt is all sweaty.

Then you've succeeded

and you can plop down

and eat your orange

and take your picture

and know that this is a sight

only for those who've earned it.

"Stay out Mom and Dad. I do not let meanease in."

The boldly scrawled sign hung at the entry to my seven-year-old daughter's room.

It left no question about where we stood.

She had recently taken her two-year-old brother under her wing, protecting him from other siblings, running to him when he cried, carrying him upstairs when he couldn't make it himself and distracting him with play when it looked like he could be getting into trouble.

"I do not let meanease in"

Now she was his defender.

He had been sent to his room for an unprovoked attack on a brother. Once alone, he stood against the wall and cried bitterly at his exile.

It was more than she could bear.

She tried to go to him. She pleaded with us to back down. Then she drew up her sign and placed it on her door.

Long after her brother had been freed, hugged and forgiven, she felt bitterly toward the "meanease" who could reprimand such a small, tender child.

She wouldn't have believed our own struggles.

I've seen how he runs to the far wall of the bedroom when the door with the impossible knob is closed to him.

I've felt how he hugs me desperately after the punishment has ended, clinging to the safe feeling of being in my arms again, wanting to be assured that I still love him even though I chastened him. And wanting me to know of his love for me.

In the years since, I have been accused with distressing regularity of being a mean mom. I am mean because I won't let my daughters go to slumber parties when I don't know the family. I'm mean when I won't let my son eat dessert before lunch. I'm mean when I require the completion of often upleasant chores.

But I was never going to be a mean mom.

I was going to be a mom who let her kids sneak samples of chocolate-chip cookie dough and who bought them each their own order of French fries.

I was going to be a mom who played games with her kids, sang lullabies and not only allowed but shared in adventures.

But I hadn't anticipated the fact that there would be things my children would want to do that were wrong, or dangerous.

And as they go to their rooms in anger or tears, I pace the floor in mine, wishing I could go easier, but knowing I can't.

Giving love sometimes means giving limits.

Teaching sometimes means disciplining.

Parenting all too often means being "meanease."

Let me go with you down the path.

Let me walk by your side

    while you walk by my side.

Let me hold your hand

    while you hold my hand.

Together, we can make any journey.

The sound

is almost deafening

The power, awe-inspiring

The beauty, captivating.

Such a vast space

Such incredible might.

I, so small, can never control it

But I can treasure it

And from it, draw strength.

He was stuffing his money and clothes back in a dresser drawer when I walked by.

"What did you have all that out for?" I asked my then-seven-year-old.

"Oh, Ben told me you didn't care about me and that I should run away, but I decided not to," he said.

"Oh," I said, trying to remember what I may have said that would lead my son and his buddy Ben (name changed to protect innocent parents) to that conclusion.

I had been working on a project all day, only vaguely aware of the kids as they paraded in at odd intervals to report on an injustice done by another sibling.

I would look up (usually), nod (if I heard it), and say something nondescript like, "Work it out."

Apparently that was an inadequate response in my son's friend's book, who said something definitive like, "Your mother doesn't care about you," and suggested alternate living arrangements.

"He said I could live in his house for a while, or bring a sleeping bag and sleep in the cave down by the creek," came the report.

"Do you know what I'd do if you didn't come home?" I asked him.

"What?" he asked, as he returned his three dollars and 48 cents to the hiding place in his underwear drawer.

"I'd search the whole countryside over, I'd call the police and make them help me, and I'd cry and cry and cry

Because I know you care

until I found you."

"Oh," he said.

There was a pause.

"Why didn't you leave?" I asked.

"Because I know you care."

Running away is not really that bad an idea.

The thought crossed my mind on days my daughter bounced in from school demanding, "What's for snack?" Not "Hello," mind you, or "Mom, I'm home!" or "Guess what happened at school," even. Just, "What's for snack?"

The time my three-year-old called me dummy in front of the other mothers at the children's museum was yet another. As was the time I'd spent hours preparing a new dish for dinner only to have my children go "Yuck," and my husband ask if I'd made rice to go with it. "Cabbage rolls are good with rice," he said with a patient smile.

But I wouldn't run away with my sleeping bag to a cave near the creek. I'd find a little cabin near the coast, where I'd spend my days out walking along the beach, listening to the mighty roar of the pounding waves, watching the beauty of the soaring ocean birds and feeling the strength of eternity. In the evenings I would read or write or think, uninterrupted by requests or demands or disagreements.

Running away would be so wonderfully pleasant.

But then I can't.

Because I know...that is I think...that is, most of the time I'm really quite sure… they really care. And I could never leave them to search or worry… or cry.

I care too.

An accident?

A product of mutant cells?

An evolution from a more resistant strain?

A coincidence of time and change?

>Such theories defy logic.

An object formed to feed the soul of man?

A work of art to inspire and enlighten?

A tender reminder of quietness amid the frantic?

A creation of a loving God?

>Now that makes perfect sense.

Insights

My son and I think there won't be time in heaven.
It seems logical that a place that goes on forever
    and that's always been there
    wouldn't worry about 9:30
    or a quarter of three.

That sounds pretty good to us.

He, who has to catch buses
    and go to music time
    and soccer practice
    and bed.
I, who must get kids to dentist appointments
    and piano lessons
    and attend school programs
    and need an alarm clock to know it's morning.

We don't think there will even be clocks in a place like that.
And to us, it sounds... divine.

It works on his tape player

"I wish we could back-forward to before it happened."

My son was feeling badly because his sister had been injured in a preventable accident that ended up requiring five stitches in her littlest finger.

It had been traumatic for all of us – the screams, the blood, the frantic preparations to get to the doctor, the big white bandage that protected the cut from moisture and dirt.

And as we sat at the dinner table thinking of all the simple little things that, if changed only slightly, would have prevented it, he wished for all of us that we could do it over again.

It works on his tape player. If he wants to hear something again, he just pushes the button with the double arrows pointing to the left, and he has a second chance to hear it.

I wish for that rewind button sometimes too.

Sometimes for big things, and sometimes even for little ones.

I was inwardly criticizing myself for something I had left unsaid during a presentation. It was a silly little thing, but I, being a silly big thing, kept thinking and rethinking how I should have said it, what the reaction would have been if I'd done it as planned, and whether or not I could call the group together again for another go at it.

Finally, as in all desperate emotional traumas in my life, I brought my husband in on my problem.

"Do you ever berate yourself over and over again for something you should have done and didn't?" I asked.

"I do berate myself," said my calm and wise spouse. "But only once and then I go on from there."

Only once and then go on.

I think I'll try that sometime.

Had anyone else done it, I would have said "no-no" sternly and nipped it in the bud.

But this was my youngest, and before I could say "no-no" and do the nipping,, his older siblings were pointing to him and laughing uproariously, encouraging him in his antics.

He was one year old, and he was taste-testing boiled eggs.

First he picked up the egg yolk, rolled it around in his fingers, and then dropped it on the high chair tray. Then he picked it up again, rolled it around some more and dropped it from a little higher off the platter.

Then he took the plunge, popped it in his mouth and popped it right back out again.

It had flunked the test.

And after one more bounce on the tray, it was tossed on the floor to join all other rejected food stuffs.

I guess it was the laughter and the encouragement that convinced him his methods were worthy of praise.

Thus they became normal procedure.

The youngest child in the family learns to do things differently than those who are born when parents are the major influence. Brothers and sisters are significant mentors when every waking moment is spent in their company.

The older children were taught not to burp out loud at the dinner table. My youngest son can choose between keeping Mother and Dad's rule, or getting some major guffaws from the crowd by ignoring it. For a natural performer, those laughs are pretty tempting, making adjustments in behavior more difficult to achieve.

While his older siblings grew up with "Eensy Weensy Spider" and the "ABC" song, his first songs were "I'm Bad, I'm Bad, You Know It" and "Who you gonna' call? Ghost Busters."

While the older children played with blocks and rattles, he was into Constructs and UNO cards.

He was taste-testing boiled eggs

But my youngest is not the only one affected by his ranking in the family.

True to birth-order stereotypes, my oldest daughter was nothing short of presidential in those early years. Friends would ask us if she "mothered" her younger siblings. It was more like she "presided" over them.

This girl was a take-charge kind of kid. There wasn't a game going on anywhere in the house that she couldn't step in and set rules that were more efficient and interesting and more to her advantage.

There wasn't a fellow sibling anywhere around that she

couldn't tell what they did wrong and why they aren't smart enough to do better.

Life on the homefront is a study in personalities, relationships, environments and reactions. I soon confirmed that as some texts suggest, middle children get very good at mediating and avoiding conflict.

When you have a president on one side telling you what's wrong with you and what to do when, and a little brother on the other side demanding that you laugh when he burps and invading your UNO games, you soon learn to get along with everybody.

Certainly birth order doesn't make the whole of an individual, but my observations confirm that where you came in affects to some extent how you are.

It was obvious from the very first words my children spoke.

My oldest already had a younger brother by the time she put a sentence together. Her first concerned phrase was "Baby c'ying." He, on the other hand, put his first words together to defend himself from his big sister. He first said, "Gimme dat."

The next child started her speaking career with "Dat's mine."

Our youngest's first phrase was also interactive.

Pointing to his brother, he said: "He did it."

Worrying has come easy

People who worry should be warned about having children.

As if there isn't enough to worry about regarding the state of the economy, the military strength of world powers and whether or not it's going to rain over the weekend, children add significantly to the number and the degree of one's worries.

I've always been the kind of person to lie awake at night wondering if I'd forgotten to turn the oven off. The day my husband started refusing to check it out was the day I decided there were better things in life to worry about – like whether a sideache meant appendicitis, whether the alarm would go off in the morning or whether I'd live long enough to see Hawaii again. Those things can be worried about without getting out of bed.

Worrying has come easy to me all my life. One of the first things I remember worrying about was that I wouldn't make it home from elementary school in time to get to the bathroom – a worry that was not totally unfounded.

Later school worries were that my nose was too long, my clothes were too old fashioned, or the wrong boy would ask me to dance.

Worriers should never take up skiing. My husband, who doesn't appreciate the fine art of worrying because he only worries once every other year, convinced me to take up skiing before we were married.

I skied all right, but I worried as well. I worried about falling off the chairlift at the bottom and again at the top. I worried about the slick roads to the lodges, losing my partner and looking stupid. I even shaved my legs before every trip to the slope so that if I broke my leg, those handsome men in the ski patrol wouldn't be repulsed when they went to set it.

When I got married my worries were compounded. I worried about how we could afford the groceries I'd just purchased, how I was going to tell my husband how much I'd just spent on groceries, and how I didn't have anything to cook for dinner despite all the money I'd spent on groceries.

When my husband was a little late from work, I worried that there had been an accident and shed a few tears of self pity. When he was a lot late from work, I worried that he had found some cute, worry-free co-worker to take out for a drink. When he was a little more than a lot late from work, I worried about whether I should call the insurance company or the divorce attorney.

Then came children.

Worries began as soon as the pregnancy was confirmed: Will I make it the hospital in time? Am I going to have twins? Will it hurt?

They got worse with a newborn: Is she eating enough? Is she sleeping too much? Will she make a scene if I take her shopping? Will her belly button remain an "outie?"

And toddlers add considerably to the list of worries: Will he hate me if I'm too strict? Will I spoil him if I'm too soft? Is he learning his alphabet fast enough?

Will the absence of a "Power Ranger" in his life affect his long-term happiness?

I don't know when it ends.

Surely not when they're 16 and driving and dating and refining their attitude problems.

Apparently not when they're on their own and changing jobs, marrying and having children, if my own mother's

example is representative.

Maybe worrying proves you have something you value.

Maybe worrying only stops when you stop caring.

Maybe worrying is a necessary part of loving.

Maybe everything will be OK, anyway.

There we sat, fat, ugly, frustrated

We were supposed to be talking about nurturing our children, but it soon became apparent they weren't the ones with the problem.

Our little support group for mothers started out discussing how compliments, consideration and appreciation build self-esteem in children, but ended up with an entirely different focus.

As it turned out, we were already doing our best to nurture our children's self-esteem.

What we weren't nurturing was our own.

No compliments. No appreciation. No acceptance. And consequently, little self-respect.

Part of the problem was our bodies. Having all gone through child-birth, we had sags in some spots and stretch marks in others.

So we told ourselves we were fat and ugly.

Part of the problem was our role. With children, we were busy from morning until night, but didn't have much to show for it.

So we told ourselves we were unsuccessful.

Part of the problem was that sometimes we'd get angry at the very children we loved most and for whom we wanted to be the very best.

So we told ourselves we were bad mothers.

And there we sat, fat, ugly and frustrated, needing badly to nurture ourselves.

There were lots of ideas – from hiring a baby-sitter so there would be time for a nap, to keeping lists of the day's many small accomplishments. But the change it seems we needed most, was the ability to stop criticizing and start liking ourselves.

Mothers are their own worst enemies.

When they're playing with their children, they feel guilty that the housework's not getting done. When they're doing housework, they feel guilty that they're not playing with their children.

They feel sure that if they'd just find the right method of discipline the kids would get along better, or if they'd just work harder the house would stay cleaner.

But transferring the child-nurturing ideas of compliments, consideration and appreciation to ourselves turned up some interesting results.

"The laundry isn't even done yet and already the kids have muddied today's clothes," became, "The laundry I wanted to do today is almost done."

"Another diaper to change," became, "Aren't I good at this after all this experience!"

It's the difference between tuna casserole and seafood fettucini ala carte.

It's the difference between arguing with your husband and discussing an issue which you see from different angles.

It's the difference between seeing the shadow and feeling the light.

It's the difference between half empty and full to overflowing.

I guess it's my job to teach them not to be so honest.

As we were waiting to be helped in a local book store, my three-year-old son whispered ever so distinctly, "Mom, look at that bi-i-i-ig man."

I nodded absently and answered, "Yes, dear," before realizing there really was a bi-i-i-ig man within eye-shot – and ear-shot.

"That floor must be really slippery," said my pre-school daughter as we sat through a performance by a nouveau dance troupe. Her explanation was as good as any I could generate to

They're too darned honest

explain the flopping and flailing during one number.

"Mom says you eat a lot," said that same daughter to my brother, misquoting a chatty aside I'd made while stocking the cupboards for his visit.

You can't lie yourself out of a corner when dealing with kids. "What I really meant was..." or "You misunderstood me..." or, especially, "No I didn't," will never help.

Not just because you don't want to tell even a white lie in front of your kids, but because no one believes an adult when put up against a child. Kids are too darned honest.

Naturally it was a child who pointed out that the emperor in the old fable had no clothes. Children are not easily fooled by what they have been told. They don't have the background of

biases and beliefs that color our adult perceptions.

They know a naked man when they see one. And an overweight one, too.

Still, honesty is not always the best policy and it is the sad lot of a parent to teach the biases and train in the sensitivities that will help a child determine when tact is better than fact.

"No thank you," when offered spinach is better than, "Yuck, that's gross."

"I'm going to play someplace else" is better than the honest, though temporary truth, "I hate you."

Yet there's something lost in replacing truth with tact. There's something open, innocent and real about saying how you really feel and what you really think despite the repercussions.

"Your car is m-u-u-u-c-h dirtier than ours," was a comment from a four-year-old girl in our carpool. That truth hurt, but got results.

After my husband and I returned from a weekend ski trip, I was again confronted with the truth.

"Do you know why Daddy and I went away together?" I asked, hoping to share some insights on developing and maintaining relationships, and at the same time make my children feel safe and secure in the knowledge their parents still loved each other and enjoyed being together.

But my son saw it differently and answered quite abruptly: "Because you want to get away from us."

"Oh," I may have said if I was a bit more honest, "that too."

After 10 years of watching and learning, growing and feeling, it was time to form some opinions.

"I don't think Dad did a very good job on Mother's Day gifts," was the first comment from my 10-year-old daughter.

She had bought me flowers and made a coupon book offering free help with baby-sitting, doing dishes and vacuuming. Her Dad had bought me hot pink gardening gloves and basketball earrings.

The earrings were her idea.

She had been shopping with him the night before the big day. She watched as he stopped at an outdoor store to pick up a few things for himself and then headed to the local drug store where the gardening gloves were selected. She suggested the earrings might be good too.

But still, when Sunday dawned, she was embarrassed for him even after I pointed out that the two of us had agreed to go easy on holiday gifts since we were splurging for a week-long trip together the next month.

Her next salvo was at me. I had just spent six hours on my half of a volunteer project when the person who was to do the other half backed out, leaving me looking at another six hours to wrap up.

My daughter had seen my labor and she sensed my frustration.

"Just tell her it's her job!" she said. "Tell her you volunteered to do half and she is supposed to do the rest and you did your part and now she is supposed to do hers."

It sounded like a reasonable response, but my empathy towards another overworked mother made me prefer to finish it on my own.

Later, after I had run up a big bill at the copy center for the same volunteer project, my daughter was beside herself.

"Mom," she said with an air of you-should-have-figured-this-out-yourselfness. "This volunteer work is no good. It takes a lot of time and a lot of money and you don't get anything back."

She's right about some things. Hot pink gardening gloves are not a very good Mother's Day gift, so next time I won't agree to "go easy" – trip or no trip.

She's right that people should do what they've committed to do, and

"This volunteer work is no good"

hopefully our experience will ensure her own dependability in the future.

There is indeed no money in volunteer work, but she may someday find that giving and doing just because someone needs you is more rewarding than giving and doing because someone will pay you.

There's a lot to learn about life.

Even after 10 years.

Fast food or gourmet

"Simpsons" on TV *or* "Kick the can" out back

Watching a video *or* listening to Grandpa tell about growing up

Flipping Nintendo controls *or* painting a picture

Exercising at the club *or* doing the housework

Cozying up to cartoons *or* curling up with a good book

Renting extra video games for the weekend *or* going camping

Disneyland *or* Glacier National Park

The movies *or* the symphony

Gameboy *or* Monopoly

Fast food *or* gourmet

Storebought *or* homemade

Shopping *or* serving

Television *or* conversation

Imitation *or* original

Artificial *or* real

What my kids like *or* what I like.

They were all bored. Each one – exceptionally bored.

No TV, no friends, no satisfactory answers to "What can we do now, Mom?"

There was nothing left to do but pull out some paper and crayons and write a book.

My seven-year-old son and eight-year-old daughter combined efforts for the project and wrote "Ninga (sic) Turtles and Dinosurs (sic)."

It was a harrowing tale of ninjas and dinosaurs in space, with helicopters, missiles, space ships and things that "icspoted (sic)." Graphic pictures filled the pages with creatures falling off ships and being hammered by bombs. Fortunately, they ended up living happily in a "land they didn't know of" that was "very beutiful (sic), it had rivers people and pretty little houses."

My five-year-old wrote her own fully-illustrated tale of a little girl who finds a baby while picking flowers one day and sails off with her in a boat.

Then it was time for a treasure hunt. Notes were hidden around the house for others to track and sticks of gum or little toys were discovered as treasures.

Then it was theater, and a dramatization of Little Red Riding Hood, complete with Mom's old red shirt for our heroine and an old brown towel for the wolf.

Then there was a puppet show. Then they played ball and before long it was time to have dinner and head to bed, exhausted.

For a boring day, it wasn't all bad

For a boring day, it wasn't all bad.

There aren't many boring days for kids or adults in today's active, ambitious, aspiring society. Too much time is required for functional, necessary, structured activities.

But when the TV's off, the friends are gone and the lists are set aside, a boring day can end up so rewarding it's exhausting.

Even for grown-ups.

It's not high cholesterol, it's not excess weight, it's not the absence of aspirin or oat bran that's killing us.

It's the waiting in lines.

We rush and run, we hurry and scurry – only to stand and wait.

At the grocery store, on the highway, in McDonald's and at the movie theater, our bodies must pause while our minds are racing to the next project, the next stop, the next accomplishment.

Those who are resourceful might read an article, start up a conversation, pick out a candy bar, practice a good argument, plan a trip away or memorize a good quote as they wait. But one thing's even better:

Sit quietly and watch.

Without looking ahead all the time, we can enjoy being the very place we are.

It's the waiting

The gooey chocolate substance inched its way down from the top shelf in the refrigerator.

It crawled over the Tupperware containing left-over soup and the cheese wrapped in plastic before dripping downward to cover the tortillas on the bottom shelf.

It was just about to the vegetable drawer when I found it.

A child's cooking experiment gone awry.

A culinary disaster, but not a crisis.

To the experienced eye of a long-time mother, this brown coating on my refrigerated food was really only a comparatively slight irritation.

It was not smelly, it was not gross, it was just gooey, and along with the help of the responsible party, I calmly set out to clean it up.

We wiped, we rinsed and we talked about what could have gone wrong, until the refrigerator was once again in order and the garbage disposal had dispensed of the disappointing dish.

It was supposed to have been a chocolate mousse pie. One of those easy little package numbers where you add a bit of butter here and a bit of milk there and your guests rave about your culinary proficiency when the credit really goes to JELL-O.

My daughter had made a similar dish with my help a few months prior. This was one she wanted to do all by herself.

But what was supposed to get the butter got the milk, and what was supposed to get the milk got the butter, and though it seems a slight error, the results were undesirable.

Inedible, in fact.

Despite extended time in the refrigerator, the crust didn't set up as filling and the filling didn't crunchy up like crust. Instead, since it had been set a bit askew in the over-full frig, rather than set up, the ingredients set out on a grand tour of the place.

That's when I came in.

I suppose the whole matter could have come to a happier ending had I participated to a greater extent in the process.

But I had been invited to withdraw, and I agreed to do so.

There are times mothers get tired of having to teach every lesson.

They get tired of reminding kids to wear coats on cold days, practice the piano for lessons and read the labels on JELL-O mixes. They get tired of saying fire will burn you, and if you hit someone they might hit you back, and if you don't go to bed on time you'll be grouchy the next morning.

Sometimes getting cold, having a bad lesson or a failed recipe, feeling the heat, the hit or the tiredness, makes a more lasting impression.

When safe, lessons from life are ever-so-much-more meaningful – and memorable.

Take strawberries, for example.

There wasn't a day that went by when I hadn't said to at least one of my

A culinary disaster, but not a crisis.

children on at least two occasions that eating too many strawberries would make them sick.

We had picked our own one morning and each child had filled his or her own personal bowl. This was a source of great pride, and they subsequently determined to eat every last strawberry in that own personal bowl.

For the first few days all was well, but when the berries started looking over-ripe, my oldest daughter (the one with the largest bowl), decided to eat a little bit harder and faster so as not to lose a single precious berry. Then my husband made strawberry shakes for dessert. Then someone gave her a chocolate bar.

Then she was awake all night with an upset stomach and when she did sleep, her dreams were of gigantic bowls of strawberries with chocolate streaming over the top.

And I will never again have to tell her not to eat too many strawberries.

And there's no need to say "I told you so."

When nature's lessons reinforce mother's, the burden of teaching lightens just a bit.

But that really wasn't the reason I didn't get angry as I cleaned the chocolate goop out of my refrigerator.

I didn't get angry because I was remembering some 20 years earlier when I learned a somewhat similar lesson in a somewhat similar way.

I had been allowed the freedom to learn on my own how to bake a cake.

It was my first cake and made from scratch, as was the norm in those days. It was my mother's birthday and we were to celebrate at my grandmother's home, and I relished the praise that would be my due for having accomplished such a task on such an occasion.

I was extremely pleased when, after combining the proper ingredients, I found that while most other chefs had to use two nine-inch rounded pans for their batter, I could pour the whole works into one.

My mother had offered me a chance to learn by experience.

And I did.

And then we got to clean her oven.

Nothing fit

A cry of frustration came from down the hall.

I looked up from my work, listened for further clues to the problem, for things being thrown or broken or any indication of pain. When there was none, I turned back and carried on.

Soon another cry rent the air – this one registering more grief than the first.

I shook my head and slowly headed down the hallway.

My three-year-old son was playing in his bedroom while the other children were at school.

He was working on a puzzle and nothing fit.

It used to be that I would rush to the rescue of such a child, patiently helping him find the right spot for each piece.

But with this child I knew better.

"It is so maddening when the pieces don't go together," I confirmed, as I watched.

Then I picked up a piece and put it in a spot where – it didn't fit!

I'd failed and he registered my failure.

I tried again somewhere else and still it wouldn't fit.

I tried again and then set it aside for later and picked up another piece.

And he watched.

One can't be too careful in dealing with kids and puzzles.

And though I had been guilty of finding faster solutions with earlier children, this time I wasn't out to impress anyone, except perhaps with a thought.

Puzzle lessons shouldn't be: "Mothers are smarter so have them do it for you," or "It's too hard for you so give up and find something else to do."

Children need lessons in: "Don't get mad or give up when you fail. Just try it a different way the next time," or "Success is all the more exciting when you've overcome a challenge to reach it."

One can't be too careful with puzzles.

"Look what I found!"

We weren't looking for shells, but the little white objects contrasting with the wet, brown sand demand the attention of anyone walking along the beach.

So the search was on.

"Mom, look at this one!" over a mussel cracked only on one side.

"Look what I found!" over a still-round sand dollar whose fragile top had caved in.

Little hands picked up the delicate creations of Mother Nature and little voices exclaimed over their beauty.

And the collections began.

One went into a pocket, others were nestled in a rolled up shirt. Some settled among friends in upside down hats or were turned over to Mom's larger hands.

It didn't matter that they weren't perfect.

Few shells that make it to Oregon's beaches are.

The battering from the rows and rows of breaking waves can do even the toughest shell damage. So they come up with a corner missing here or a top missing there or a crack down the middle.

Still, the children loved them.

They were beautiful, even when broken.

It took me a while to see that beauty. I was a holdout for the perfect shell, even if it meant buying it from the local tourist shop for $1.50.

After hours along the shores of the Pacific Ocean, I would have one tiny shell or none at all.

But this year something changed. This year I saw those broken shells differently.

Even in pieces, the color, the design, the shape, the story became significant to me.

I picked up one, then another, then more.

I turned them in my hands, felt their strength even after the pummeling, saw their intricacies and cherished their endurance.

I brought them home, placed them tenderly in my most shapely glass bowl and set them in a prominent place to remind me of something new:

Beauty can still be found in those broken but surviving.

Perfection is not a prerequisite for appreciation.

It is not necessary to be perfect to be loved.

If I could end every day with a sunset…

If there were no clouds to hide sun…
No trees or houses to block my view…
No meetings to do…
No errands to run…
No dinner to stew…
No tasks to be done…

If I could end every day with the sun…
I would end every day… renewed.

Art can change things

I have sunsets in my den.

Sunsets I witnessed and recorded on film, that bring a certain serenity even when bills are being paid or words don't come as easily as they might.

I have flowers and gardens framed in my living room.

Flowers that are always in bloom, gardens that never need weeding, plants that never wither and die in the cold.

I have a picture of a woman walking through a wind-swept meadow hanging in my laundry room.

Everyone knows that a woman walking through a wind-swept meadow is thinking about life and love. And that's what I do while ironing. I think about life and love, and the poster on the wall helps carry me to a place far away from little boys' size eight shirts and little girls' size ten dresses.

In the cupboard where I keep my phone books is a quote from Johann Wolfgang von Goethe: "He is happiest, be he king or peasant, who finds peace in his home."

Just next to it is a cartoon of a frazzled woman in line at the grocery store with a couple of toddlers swinging from the aisle post and a baby or two nestled in between the diapers and wipes in the cart.

It reminds me of me.

Art can change things. It can take the frazzled and make them funny. It can take the mundane and make it magnificent.

A dear friend was between generations, caring for an ailing mother and a daughter bedridden with pregnancy, and wearing out her goodness in service. I took a photograph of this friend as she held a sleeping granddaughter. Though it was no masterpiece, it allowed her to see the beauty in her service. The contented face of the child who loved and trusted enough to sleep in her arms was suddenly a visible reward for all the worries and all the time and all the tiredness.

It wasn't work to care for them after all. It was love.

Life can sometimes be tiring – like when you're meeting everyone else's needs but your own. It can sometimes be frustrating – like when you can't watch a sunset because you're needed elsewhere. It can sometimes be boring – like when you have to iron yet again. It can sometimes be embarrassing – like when you're in line at the grocery store with rambunctious kids.

But looking at life through different eyes – those of an artist or writer, a philosopher, photographer, or even a cartoonist – can bring a different perspective.

By allowing us to step back and be outside looking in, we can see things we may otherwise have missed.

We can then see life as fun or exciting or challenging – or even beautiful.

Maybe life really is.

It might not change the world.

One little rock, thrown as hard and as far as I can throw.

It might not change the world.

But I like to try.